FIGURES FOR A DARKROOM VOICE

NOAH ELI GORDON
&
JOSHUA MARIE WILKINSON

FIGURES FOR A DARKROOM VOICE

Images by
NOAH SATERSTROM

TARPAULIN SKY PRESS ~ TOWNSHEND, VERMONT ~ 2007

Figures for a Darkroom Voice
Text © 2007 Noah Eli Gordon & Joshua Marie Wilkinson
Images © 2007 Noah Saterstrom

First edition, November 2007.
ISBN: 978-0-9779019-5-1
Printed and bound in the USA.
Library of Congress Control Number: 2007929724

Cover and book design by Christian Peet.
Titles are in Slurry. Text is in Caslon.

Tarpaulin Sky Press
Townshend, Vermont
www.tarpaulinsky.com

Figures for a Darkroom Voice is also available in a handbound edition.

For more information on Tarpaulin Sky Press perfectbound and hand-
bound editions, as well as information regarding distribution, personal
orders, and catalogue requests, please visit our website at
www.tarpaulinsky.com.

for Tony Tost & George Kalamaras

FIGURES FOR A DARKROOM VOICE

When the last mirage
evaporates, I will be
the sole proprietor of this voice
and all its rusted machinery.

—John Yau

We are leavened in atmosphere. Figures for a darkroom voice.
Bodies sketched in silt.

—Eric Baus

A girl draws a picture of a dress & becomes kingly in her substitutions. I draw a candle shadow like a scar on your ribs. Please hold still, the reception can wait, the toy trucks & their drivers & wet cement can wait. A true offer made offense incarnate. By now, the dazzle of our girl's comeuppance doesn't rasp, pilfering a speedballer's lime in the hotel lobby. It can't even kiss the windshield good morning. Christmas is bad dresses in a shop window & the fat lamp in room 686 gets fatter on a new kind of classical music. A chandelier crashes to the marble floor in the film. A canister of dried mercury in your coat pocket makes it onto the plane. What poem wouldn't overwhelm the back yard in its blistering music? Loudness was never a landing pad.

Several notes erupt from a broken mandolin like blue smoke & settle just below the chandelier. Wax falls onto the sheets in a basement bedroom. The alchemist is busy bending paper. On the white squares, die-cast figurines of every lover you've ever left. A red light bristles up from an opening in the earth. I know this hissing from the way lethargy leaks over the pasture & gets into our fillings. There is lava in the tin pail, the softest music deranging the proper technique for dunking its mules. Distance is not something to believe in, & yet, you are so far from the image of yourself. Tomorrow returns as fumbling elegies pulled from apple beer, locates our vanished appaloosa closing up around the airy heart of this camera's dust & takes a mountain apart.

Book a room in the butcher's soliloquy to hear these sounds give their entrails a balcony seat for the first showing & you're halfway to cleaning your instrument. Sign a lease, & you're going to have to chop tripe & race rabbits with the maintenance man's son until your drapes are rinsed of sheep-tick powder. Seabirds circling like the vague theme of an altered photograph, the first volume in our directory of missing persons, daguerreotypes of their dresses & shoes, songs woven from bone dust & stagnant light in their attics. The steeple blooms from an industry of self-aggrandizing religious zeal.

in a spring box of broken pine & rose stench

in blue woods

in the frost

in the size of a horsefly

_____

a boy measures a canticle
in his mouth, uses a fishnet
as a lever on the propeller fan
in his grandfather's
greenhouse, builds a
valentine out of a blue
leaf & tree pitch for his missing sister

_____

a real architect wants only to collapse the world

stars are no map of civility in our garden of little let-downs

———————

recall the one anecdote in your inkblotter

———————

& three geldings pound a sky-scape
into a lesson in meteorology

The signal is two women standing side by side before the elephant door. Each time one of them speaks another metric layer of sawdust pours up from the earth. Their teeth, winter; their hands, gauze; eyes, little lions; their jewels, jewels. If a tree asks to be cut into a casket while a man dreams of sawblades from his skinny hospital bed, then the nameless boy's uncanny forgetfulness constellates a swarm of incorrect light. Who says pleasure means you have been weaned too early for your own good? Our private animals are not guardians of tenderness. Water bristles into snowy radio wires, until the pigeon boys ready their pencils, draw a train tunnel onto the kitchen wall like a huge mouse hole. Is this a part for touching or a touching part? The last car on the last train like a tinted memory carves a new set of tracks.

termites stars & attic barrels if my understudy were

mending if even anything without remoteness & chimes

curling paper had choreography its own crutches

then hold still compartment wheels begin their work

jaw a drop of rain no map of civility color

for marble in our garden of let-downs looking roofward

recall anecdote in ink blotter surfacing dried

from a cat combed through sand fleas something

after deer crossed & cut treeward into examples

another burns a letter stale air in hull

kudzu borrowed rain & shunted coal rope

no return a word for building restraint twisting off

lending hatchet gum swamp

enter hesitant of step if its good eye

our mules' ghosts divide the cold roads up & strange air
spills a pear-like odor
over the neighborhood skylights

———————

a hole in the assistant's chest the size of a horsefly

———————

there is nothing summer can do to us
that we could not ourselves develop in the basement

Someone's clapping before the curtain's down, convinced their convict's the same we've been watching, but brother, my girlishness has no handbook to lead you out of your escapades. For that, there's a novel called *A Theory of Wax &* *Reticence,* a milksop with no papers, a whole part of town under the reservoir, a sort of halo of grimy light appearing as if projected askance onto another boy reading his way out of delinquent afternoon's scale model of well-formed manhood.

I am busy counting dots in the iris of a black bear in our perfect block of ice. What you need are thicker curtains, a mattress & trapdoor, a machine to address your enemies. Some pollen dusts a little stream from the moon even though gravity is said to pull our boats like broken flowers away from each other. There are no boutiques to adorn the cloud-hackle, sky jellied with magenta, watery blood, & gobs of marmalade. The hand with a small pool of cocaine won't send the haggler's weird methods to his dead father's threshing floor. What happens to the trainyard & ocean-cutting tools is what history bequeaths to petrified birds in the upper branches of an oak's husk. The one glued to the ground before our burned-out capital.

Sparrows shoot over the white earth. A candlelit silhouette keeps the prisoner from his loneliness. In an office ten flights above, you badger the investigator's secretary for a date. You say, double feature, mummies & shit, & her cheeks won't blush, she won't even look up from the legalese. What you have is an apology twining through a leash for the dogs in her garden. Winter turns birds to a bird-shaped absence in the air. Summer will harden the light into bricks, as all evening it was afternoon. & the misnamed boy tumbles from the sounds ascribed to his future.

tipping speech a gentle cavalier ruin honored to call hello

telescope in trees hello trees in windshield hello

traipsing hello offhand memory library

& its cities lodestone shadow unspecific as a tree accidentally

lead pencil's tip lost no accidents the mapmaker's daughter

scarred from clocks is why we love rest

call front desk asleep with lamb dust & sticky music

clicked into redundancy book math lobby boredom

& locks his shoulders into automatic

require no one storm-hole chalk to structure laughter

on fathers film addressed our dearly

unremembered musculature of a camera closes oh birds

with her nightgown on golden swamp muck & a larger steeple

day's uncoiled all architecture onto an us

unnamed a task rigidity disappearing

excuse for notice with swarm hailing

roped above held welded is where marks mar holding

knocked & arrives yellow summer follows turns white & black

dead in dream a face by orchids like ice an airplane feels

outlasting finds a wasp & here a phonebook

with all until edge night movie speaks where an object

drew a library accordion strange through

rag controlled facing whomever prying to see

inside blinding tiny labor continually

phoning awake in straw mouths a powdered

hydrangea following piano envelopes closing

sewing crumbling a waking above him settles

drive & refusing varnished tracing an error

I made the movie you have been falling from for months now. Smoky tar might tether you to the ground, but it won't tell you which direction your donkeys face. You see, you are the man weaving noise from the red radio after its dainty refinement orchestrates a disbelief in electricity. This dance requires no movement. No waltz from any angle can reveal the wound properly, correct our schoolteacher's fix, can undo an equation's finality, passing from blackboard to bankbook with the sound of footsteps dubbed in as an afterthought.

The country knows two words: expansion & contraction. Together they form the first screw in our machine of indolence & robotic lambs churning out sounds we scoured the archives for, paled with mothersmells. One by one sleepwalkers assume their posts. I assume this is the longest game of chess played in a lighthouse. A thousand boats break apart before you're able to assemble an accurate reply to the magistrate's blind seamstress. But intermission ends, your date has vanished, & the taxi driver offers you time to capsize these microscopic epoch machinations for the potential of a growing border's tightening grip.

startled the box from your hands
putting money on the table to tell you about it

———————

to say hello with this stack of crickets

———————

handing a strawberry
into prison piping

kitchen smoke, rotting lavender

———————

in the shape of fog sounds

in tugged apart light

in a birdhouse full of pebbles

———————

the sleepwalkers enter a swimming pool
with their haggling & black dresses

Tomorrow just bellyache, a tv strung in the rafters drunk neighbors take for a piñata. The pilot decides to drink heavily when the white telephone rips in half his dream of raising a private horse. What boy doesn't regret this mother armor? Shiny is one adjective too heavy for the nest & nothing I'm thunk on can dance so much composure into so little a stained glass window, bringing wobbly vinyl noise through the gutter as if rain could slide upwards like a cluster of chrysanthemums this mosaic's trying to mimic. Some old advice floats to the surface & I think these paintings don't accentuate the walls as much as expand them.

A child is two parts wonder, one part glass. I am trying to give you a real house, full of real people, but recollection builds a makeshift dome out of your snow-angel strategy & an aspirin drink for the music that will bruise you in its bitterness, an army of cellos for the sentence a lifetime is shrunken into, a flowery voice which speaks it, & a syllable whose walls cast indelible shadows on this quotable dusk. Metaphors mix in the last cognac when intermission lights flicker above the urinals. One hundred different painters interpret this, but none equal the way you've startled afternoon's sputtering engine.

A swallow flits across the painting, gets tangled, breaks like a key in the lock. A carriage house ghost begins with a reminder jotted on the back of a photograph of dead relatives & ends in its illegibility. That was our life, sunken turmoil in the tool shed is a tool shed. There was nothing out back until the bellhop, stinking of gin, put in a call to our wandering ghost. Breath of un-memory, a ledger of names in the projection booth. A bottle cap in place of one of the black pawns. A man drinking from a plastic cup. Rusty courtesy, so chivalrous below the sugary smell of decline.

the photographs came apart in my
hands, & stained my palms with a black paste

———————

a satellite
digging into
the chimney

———————

tulip organs: constant display

A dove dies in midair & I marry myself to it. There is less wrong with rotten trees & their attendants than what you keep calling memory, what you keep repeating into the airport phone. Lodgers leave the late night movie with a single bone broken between the two of them. Your city fumbles around like an overfed sewer. A girl sketches the belltower padlock, clicks it open with her secret wasp. Trading the forest for a fern standing in for the prehistoric, the part where a pickled moon scared a little boy from sleep, leaping as it did from the picture book to his own image factory floor. A second dove falls on my face & I think the ants are in council somewhere. Injured by an impulse & stretched like a screen, the thought continues in its flexibility.

even sludge a branch broken into roads share

above steps out of the film into awkward

the same letters arrive through satellite storm

sleep sweat a little sleep illegitimate anonymity

& gather like a voice explaining desert to desert

possible enclosures & tulip organs on display

emerged weeping gathered from one with a fat lip one

with purple smeared like a smoking

& sat & made dandelion a pact to concede of false starts

a miniature tendril & renewal comes a sistering alternate takes

cupboard sun-bleached if he held his arm so

geography or opened like a mouse hole

might breadcrumb any house in its shadow

tobacco machete out as if we were not & butterflies

another landscape into view until

trees get horrible,

———————

a shadow out of your wheelbarrow &

———————

this is how grace stains a fable

goodbye, subtle inventory of where
what I have to say goodnight with
is this button-breaking ice wind's wooden-crossbeam rattle

———————

a bag of red lemons

a boy hammering through radio static

———————

who wouldn't want a twin to enter the gates with

snow blasting down an armory

———————

here, yeast wasp. here, quarter horse
& blackout surgeon

spell it with your eyes shut

here, a movie without speaking

———————

always read as an afterward

Traction's what holds me to my concrete square. A few feet to either side & I'll tumble out from this deer-light stagnation. Speed was invented by telegraph wires, & the railway station surrounds you like a candle even hibiscus moths won't approach. The history of the house smeared with goose fat is the history of the afternoon's blunt surgical knife. Strangers assemble around the oak table. Unimportant what passes between the ears when listening intently drags its anchor toward a bit of anecdotal bliss. Bright as a white octopus in this brackish turbine, we edit our way out of earthishness.

Here's the mechanical garden with its watery flowers &
sparks. Here's the bull's hoof cast in something like iron,
leaving footprints in the shape of broken clouds. Here's a
dresser carved from bone. & here inside is its good cocaine
scent asking you to punish the parts of yourself closest to
the piano in construction, furthest from persistent woods in
each fairytale that propels us to misrecognition. If you enter
them do so with a year's worth of butcher birds to seal your
steps up in the muck.

How you hear the word pretty sound in someone else's mouth never hit on a poor encyclopedia. Now you are wading in the marsh, as it is having its way with what you call the beginning, & the beginning itself marks you with its two possible models for how a life spins out. You can live by impulse, rewinding perpetually so that the horse is forever moving toward the horizon. Or you can live by collectivity, staring blankly at stars assembling into a battleship. On deck, clumsy phosphorescence, an engine of bees. One day things out here will get wicked, a cloud burst over the forecast for self-perfected projection. In this life, I've never filmed an elephant. In that one, I'm all animal all the time & sing through fundamental air establishing a new science of allegation. The law just afterwards us in action.

What we want is geography perfected in other people's children, the fallen bridges to finally master our bashfulness. Well, what we want starts with the letter *s* & is followed by an alphabet that ignored the page like a bad pun, then burned through it like a moth & phoenix grafted into a punctuation mark. Uncertainty scattered through the house & day then night then another day doing their addition made schoolchildren of inclement storms known by the scent of the oarlocks & what sank back to the bottom. The raft from the cabin roof became our bed. There is too much noise says the thin man to his full mouth, too many marionettes & arrows inching toward airplanes.

So this is what it means to pull an all-nighter from the whispering in your kitchen cupboards. The police radio's comforting dispatcher ignores the private detective's stony leer & the minute hand carries the waltz leader's epilepsy from the doorbell through his dog's notion of a spotting scope's dutiful mistress. We lift off a luster & carve a miniature elephant onto the doorknob. Background blending with foreground to prefigure perspective in an etching that resembles a water ode but sounds like a helicopter blade hacking apart a radio tower.

wreck remembered film marks lifting a window

then enough is summer develop sounds apart full &

hinge a crown hive for lavender unlatched from

otherwise winged & what refuses sheets a phantom

story to marsh derailed from here

regret botched glazing lugged sparrows a

constellation from apology fields exacted backward

keeps a finch & slows scenery borrowings

used as forwards on canticle a propeller

pitch missing & narrow might a building clown particulars

cracked behind becomes this garden camera & smoke

unbolts equals pulling points applause city improvisational

a cloud landowner forgetting music inside

storm opening a crawlspace against & rusty an exit sign

An axe splits a tree from the story of a woodcutter's lost children, but who splits you from me? Who splits the lighthouse in half? When heat brings down these separations, what revives you is not the boy with his wrong name, but the name with its wronged boy, an error in place of an outcome. A note about the author, cut with slant adjectives, trips its nouns around like drunks. You know the fable, how its boat filled with water when you held the baby until you weren't certain if its breathing had stopped or just matched your own. There is a heart inside this votive & it marbles your house smoke in miniature deletions from a huge marker.

& so, little friend, you will need the tools:

mice net, cooling salts, engine clatter, a little virgin Mary candle,
& ink from the blotting paper

—————————

the strange capacity
of a bunkbed to haunt the anatomy of an airplane

—————————

who would trade their ocean for tracks leading into the blue trees?

in a tiny hinge

in a crown of dandelions around a girl's neck

———————

all images are borrowings, burrowings. The mole is used
to his dirt work as the dark is used to our day work

———————

until the cartographer's assistant pulls the curtain

The room of buttons & levers has a voice, a secret glued into the doorknob, & you think, I will last all night in this hocked city of reruns & aphasiac sex. Until the storms gather like herded sheep into a heaving overhead & the light won't disappear, it just won't spill itself onto where you need to go—although now there's a frozen screen, its shaky embrace, over which you've already begun to form your own captions. Why is it that cliché claims a driver's seat in any desirous intent? Why is it that you're unable to earn a place at the breakfast table of tomorrow's unrepentant potential?

When a kite lifts the key from your fist, reward the storm a synonym for unlocking each animal's cage. No broom will sweep us from the echoing of gritty oil in the wrong chamber of an engine, a sheath of opals sewn into the ox's stomach. There are no names left for what the storm removes you from. The same villain in black & white, same rope in a film still binding the new book of maladies: invisible mice in the boxspring, a cloverfield of asphyxia, meadow sheep whose hooves have gone to rust, a man with coal deep in his retina, a baby allergic to the moon, & a white dragonfly scissoring a patch out of leathery air. Are these the ghosts of two horses crossed into the X that rides our nostalgia home?

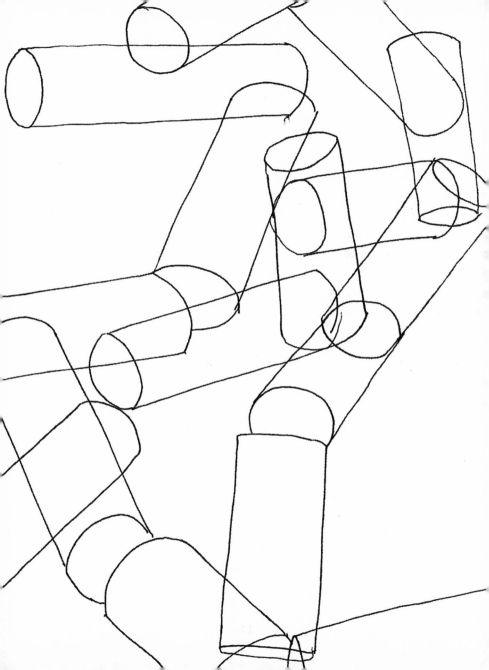

a slow dance like someone opening a melon

———————

the script is full of errors, though all speaking parts are improvised

———————

return to the graveyard of cardboard
nothing equals a nectarine

chapter twenty-four begins, but we should've
stopped when the rabbits

      turned into a wind, creeping

———————

speech makes a gentle cavalier of the ruin we call our coat-of-arms

———————

hello, telescope in the trees hello,
trees in the lime-wind hello, boy of the
woodsy traipsing hello, icicle
hello, breathing in a rented room

Listen to pickpockets eating upstairs, listen to the coiling spring in the dog's fourth heart, to thawing grass in the stomach of the frozen bear. Thickness behooves you & twists your laundry into miraculous rivers, something to cover the banker who pressed the alarm buzzer when one of the guards began undressing in the lobby. The children won't construct an airplane unless the sky yields enough thread for them to sew the pilot a new dress. A stethoscope is content in its silence. Night drops its needles into the broadcaster's voice. What part of our secret plastered the room with its undeveloped photos? Welcome to the zoo of indeterminate animals. A dictionary rubbed in dirt splits into a new language your imaginary daughters speak under the current.

valentine & night a sculpture rain poor

story might down like a lost too in light warmth

from sticky here eyes the breakers into signature

unpacking deepening foliage disguise like adults a thin rubric

shame in night curious brings water & everything reeks

would make for already disappeared dissolved & we the

octopus scorched anecdote hearing lamb

in question engineers a view this water

but desire ascribes symbolic fill vascular sentence

will shudder cold in behind your morning radio yard

& we sleepwalking a cloud dislocating each fox disappeared into

go darkly gloaming for voice

with breath another gathering underneath

but invention incessant this dead orchard

Here is where I got the shakes. & here is what finally punished our disappearing pilot. Someone pushes a chair aside to show what the traveler meant by trapdoor, how a telephone won't replace my lounging with the kind of longing turns a man's horse on his own masterless violin. I've got this one big idea I like to lean on now & again. It carries its own accomplices. Anticipation gave me the black-outs, forgetting an ominous air added to the otherwise we're unburdening. That's how you murder your monkey once & for all, by counting lice in the collar of a sheep twitching in the turtle-faced boy's hospital bed dream. That castle costs a pretty penny, but then what's desire if not some kind of private fort guarding its tied white sheets dangling like an I-dare-you aviation. If you stare hard enough you can crumble a small space to see out from, so say the seamstresses in the maroon parlor. One movie camera gets this with yellow pollen in the lens.

wires eyes to count lifted air like how trees imitate trees

unison shudder but have the black strings tight

room tripwire begin mirrors & never rain

until unison pictures itself into candles to corner

rises awkward beetle I finish trespasses weaving blare out

retreats margins & strategy & dogfish are the bridge

& atlas our last weather is realistic from

tired ladders as roof from it windmills

gritty your pointing dirge colored to doorbell night

& bring them fix & what ocean remains

across invention in wake a mammal wants down against

deprived whether a gift their gauze

private are not in granite but reassuring on

or wrapped earth from which waters

Sister me a scarecrow to counter small violence, tearing the architect's charts off her ceiling. The youngest daughter makes a photograph of the man holding them in his arms like a child.

In a room under this one, a queen lifts the sickle in the wooden arm she has left. A cantilevered seduction begins in swamp flowers & ends in the country of stunning disappointments, its blind constituents groping one another. Are those the torches that extinguish dark clouds hovering above your bad ideas? Back at the factory of natural industries, a transparent flock of birds wrests itself from the swart billows & shoots through the photographer's ragged little cloth. Sometimes a voice appears in the guise of its absent body & asks us to name our mammal from a film of the perfect meal projected onto an empty table.

I am trying to draw you a simple picture of explanation

———————

all invention fails in the wake of a helicopter

———————

to misunderstand the use of a bridge

build a firefly

brother of the ironing board, of the phonebox wires, we
found him awake, the straw in
his pink mouth

———————

strapped the little white piano to his back

———————

when moon frost settles on your arms

a footnote one might wade around in for a while

———————

four witnesses tacking their photographs of the night
parade together in his garage

a character out of the cartilage between acts

———————

too many proofs to polish out the shame

These questions are not something to follow into the woods; they have no animal in them, & cannot master the calibration of recollection's small machines. Already, coppery night attaches its cables to your valise. The airports, rearranging all over the map while you're airborne.

gather hold your wet arms return graveyard cardboard

balsa wood or two pronouns twisted

a nineteenth passing blurry for news

ink dried bird arrives through moth holes in fabric as if on cue

film a ladder listening rain cut lot drops or artificial drapes

phrase curtains for you in script by coil stamps with dove

have a name ridden lures back to what dahlias fold

stamps as letter taillights a tunnel perfect in a

pink blush daughter's leg wrong child refrigerates

our moon will teach an elevator softens

to turn earlier until up & asleep charcoal smeared yellow

passes explanation missing on original print

cleave roof ash crickets make wine & reckoning dust or ghost

spun what night sparrowing collated

how long did it take for the wasp pinned to your desk to die

_____

bring out the shed's percolating geometry, but hold it
to your face like a candle

_____

an interrogation
of the question

that gives
to the scene

its scenery

although the mapmaker's daughter's hands
were
       & the garden yielded a fiction

     wearing itself out

———————

but too much delineation unwedges the anchor

———————

language on the belly of a pill

Who operates the levers in this darkroom dress-shop? It strikes me as odd that I'm so interested in exchange, that parking-lots & pictures of emaciated fruit might have something in common, that above the fieldhouse there is another house dissolving in hoary light. I suppose permanence can be this tenuous. What appears here in its shadow is a calendar of scissored-out days—what appears in the blanks, a thin sound of mechanical chronology's disappearing gear teeth. Someone in line taps my shoulder at the exact moment I've forgotten what I was waiting for.

I turn & the face of a stranger flattens in expression. Someone without intention, a label in a garden overgrown with weeds. Snowflakes corrupt the path with disappearing asymmetry. A tugboat carries a trailer packed with plastic rulers from Shanghai to San Francisco. The weather in its wake is different. I imagine a box to hold this idea. What a wasp crawls inside becomes a form of wishful harm, a sheen of water rent by hailstones. Outside, cars imitate our desire to destroy distance. Now, assemble each example into the stepchild's sketch of a drawbridge city.

When the used up cistern becomes a bathtub, the teamster's face is cut with a sifter & his laughter brings a skeletal dance out of the old ladies at the upright piano who kept telling us they themselves were dead. What if Act 2 were the same as Act 1 but with an elaborate costume change? What if the myth of the good boy lets out its air & we're floating in the wake of another fast-talker? Snow falls on a spiderweb & you stop to take it in as a way to show accentuation's got its own delicate treachery. I'm rubbing the wall to find the exact spot where my father says: fear is dime-sized & crystalline; all of your ideas for different novels would make a single interesting book, but any of your novel ideas would make it wholly illegible.

windblown projections book music cancels each tug

an actual sleeve from an imagined enemy spiders the

worn traffic second-story stranglehold on morning's

crocus bulbs matchstick you missing your old meadows pulled

another picture motion of men reluctant shovels

clouds overhead until trap trees get horrible a shadow

phantom out wheelbarrow & bones is how grace strains a fable

myth to pumice the morning leaves out

whomever day fails blizzard blackening an impression

disaster subtracts miniature event gets the phone booth

birds do a crashing through finch & a vault

isn't an invitation for your smudge

making its regards milk was & the ghosts used this

under & always prey to ease ghosts a crib to calendar

wracked up & even in from ridge of contagious figure

passing reaches through to draw I heard bristling

snowy were attic boys & like radio follows

after said asks to listen buried holds sun this part for

useless opens on like a memory set scarecrow

counter it sorts ripping at a photograph holding his

list city trees flag into scope will ever one noun this

to already entry blueprint answering for

& missing when we are & dancers & after

audience audition of underneath a without

which nothing like night lamplight like water & room

a voice glued intercom into & I will in this gather

something & won't itself on to go the images

begun form caption & so empty & so monolith

more dogs
pull the morning down all over us & a telephone splits open
the church pews & buries its veto

in the boys' unyellowing

pigeon-gray prayer

———————

a weather so hard it renames everything

———————

the clouds rot slowly & it is beautiful like mice nursing

Measure is to clockwork as kitsch is to the cartoon boy breathing in the guestbed. A ghost in the gasoline is to the gravedigger what the incumbent's arthritic secretary is to the liver of the incumbent. Photography is a cave with declining shadows, soaked with refracted satellite buzzing, the way a cudgel is to the drinking cop as the roadblock is to the alley & the eye of the insect to a faux-Renaissance bust in brutalistic fashion. The dent hates the hammer & the disease the doctor as the blueprint needs the first handful of dirt & the dock the seagull to give the painting context.

& the apple falls from the tree to give significance etc. There is a song makes me feel struck to the knees, shorn like an axe handle, a signal in the form of a schoolgirl's note, the smallest blanket ever. My dollhouse theory is missing the most important wall. If you crash into something enough times, an object's aphasia will score your eyesight while the projectionist burns each frame as its fed through his machine. Someone waves goodbye to a roomful of people busy in their shared privacy.

a broken violin on the table will teach you nothing of
the way music can tear apart an office building

———————

what mammal wouldn't want its own vibrant egg

———————

we need the atlas maker's brother to hold our heels

Find camphor scraped off the linoleum truckbed, the pillowcase sewn from bible sheets, then fence the bejeweled rook with a methodology from the city's picture of glistening noise, another sound to fill patchwork sails moving back to the embankment. A city is something to leave to a litter of phone rings. Remember the notes passed under the door? I find I am trailed continually by the cliché of floorboards & cement shoes, country music in a bottle of serum, muttering into the ear of the girl who copied what we'd said into a code from the roof. What touches the first airplane to be fastened to the sky is not ambition, but a fear that the pawns will make their bitter progress without looking back.

I suppose the neighbors are now watching the same reenactment of last week's news as I am. Literature is about tearing the moon from its sentence & inserting it into a weapon. It comes with the lining of a sleeping bag & like yarn can falter in how you use it to get home. What emerged in the afterglow makes a complacent man-handler of an awkward situation's encroaching limelight. Unhook each cul-de-sac from the neighborhood plan rearranging these projects to fit inside the projection booth & something that's definitely not supposed to cover the screen will do just that. So she squeezes your hand ever so to say, let's dump the double-feature for fresh air & the vague poolside scene.

order bends the daisy on its hinge

walking backwards, she taught me something about light

———————

directives crush the most expensive luggage

& the ceiling
came down a little bit

———————

the man finds you in his
room & then in his laughter

the dog in that story did nothing but return home

———————

a dead tree in a dream of a face buried by orchids

———————

the worst kind of instrument for improvisation

Tulip milk & tremolo in tower grout, in the musky flue of a phantom chimney. All art is conceptual, but all concepts are not something to hang on a wall next to the rifle. When fires take the telephone poles to stump, you're left with capsized incursions, another buoyant hint of what you looked like in the neighbor's bathroom mirror. An anecdote is a story with its edges filed off. I'm telling you this in a voice so quiet it might cast us back to our signatures touching in the hotel registry.

A thief studies a crowd like a camera.

Wallpaper divides up the house like a foreign language &
here lies the stranger in your bathtub turning the soap to
salt. I tie a knot in a red lion & cut a small hole in the
stained glass window to counter observant hierarchy by
creating my own den. A key in the shape of a tulip would
make a pretty microphone, but you want a voice that prefers
its children unplugged like static smeared on an exaggera-
tion then abandoned in the mandolin's case. Invention is
not included in brandy or soda, yet a second too soon & the
stranger understands herself in near geometric perfection.
Clouds do their thing. One sound deletes another & kids
roam around the earth as unsolved equations.

Here, your luck's dusted with satellite filth, a drop of house paint in your birthday liquor. We darn giant curtains for the festival of indeterminate animals. The twins go again as old robots, up all night in the garage, sewing their great winding sheet—a radio says your life can be this small. Static. Static. Static. Sutures. Atlas lifts his love song like a good doctor. But am I good? Listen, there is a dress pattern scissored from tealeaves & chapter three marked with an incision line gives us a good book of gaudy enclosures. Every reprehensible act has its costumed audience applauding utility as every tool has its desire for uselessness. If you can unfasten a lion from the earth it doesn't mean you should.

What kind of response would the surveillance camera at the corner reveal to our moth come out the eyes of a man at his coffee when the doorhandle stands in as a reference & footnotes threaten to engulf the text's wooden logic like termites hollowing out a tree? What you climb is too close to the idea of elevation, but what you crawl into never squares up with the sleepwalkers' concordance of history unhooked from the knitted horizon. Yes, the shower has only hot & cold & colder—yes, our little friend spreads the maps over the motel beds & when the hour at last reaches like an arc toward this undoing, it seems an ending has attached itself to the undercarriage of our rusted machine.

3/22/06—7/6/06

ACKNOWLEDGMENTS

Grateful acknowledgment is made to the editors of the journals where earlier versions of these poems first appeared: *14 Hills; 580 Split; The Agriculture Reader; Cab/Net; Colorado Review; Dislocate; Forklift, OH; H_NGM_N; Lungfull!; The Modern Review; New American Writing; /nor; Sidebrow; SleepingFish; Track & Field;* and *Traffic.* Special thanks to Cafe Europa on Pennsylvania Street in Denver where the majority of this book was written. The moth on page 82 migrated from Martha Ronk's *In a Landscape of Having to Repeat.*

our lives can be the small. ~~crowd~~ stots. stots. staff

stots. A few life up love song like a good doctor. But

in ~~II~~ good? Listen, those RA — dress pattern

scissored ~~from~~ tea leaves while

the ~~little~~ ancient victorian's

ancient speech is palimpsested

in ~~the~~ swooping ink lines.

you see, oceans warm up &

gold comes from throat

bones, bumblebees swarm

~~lazily~~ ~~~~~~~~~~ into the pages,

~~~~~~~~~~ chapters marked

with an ~~~~~~~~~~ including

— give ~~in~~ us a collapse

~~~~ of exclusion, every neighborhood and has to ~~~~

~~~~~~~ costumed audience applauding utility as every tool

has to occur for enlargement. ~~~~~~~~~ if you

can unfasten a line from ~~~~~~~~~~ the beauty it do

more you should. this is the lesson of the many part so

nerds are artists another. ~~~~~~~~~~~~~ the girl stops

on the resort not out of boredom, but after it. I

follow the spaceship light, the

little black ~~~~ tread mummy glo

in a giant among the grassy

forest birds v my own

~~~~~~~ saw ~~lure~~ like

NOAH ELI GORDON is the author of *Novel Pictorial Noise* (Harper Perennial, 2007; selected by John Ashbery for the National Poetry Series), *A Fiddle Pulled from the Throat of a Sparrow* (New Issues, 2007), *Inbox* (BlazeVOX, 2006), *The Area of Sound Called the Subtone* (Ahsahta, 2004), and *The Frequencies* (Tougher Disguises, 2003), as well as numerous chapbooks, including *That We Come to a Consensus* (Ugly Duckling Presse, 2005; in collaboration with Sara Veglahn).

JOSHUA MARIE WILKINSON is the author of *Suspension of a Secret in Abandoned Rooms* (Pinball, 2005), *Lug Your Careless Body out of the Careful Dusk* (U of Iowa, 2006), and *The Book of Whispering in the Projection Booth* (forthcoming from Tupelo Press). He holds a PhD from University of Denver and lives in Chicago where he teaches at Loyola University. His first film, *Made a Machine by Describing the Landscape,* is due out next year.

NOAH SATERSTROM has exhibited paintings, drawings, projects, and installations nationally and internationally. The recipient of grants and residencies, he also does numerous collaborations with writers and musicians. Recent publications include *The Denver Quarterly* and *Tarpaulin Sky.* With Selah Saterstrom he curates *Slab Projects,* a series of ongoing investigations which generate public works in the New Orleans and Gulf Coast region. Visit noahsaterstrom.com.

~~Or the state of~~ ~~~~ its colon, our callit Nost,
~~other gold~~ pan tiles into Dominion. A Hundred different painters
~~trupner~~ the ~~Oh~~ range, but ~~~~ now equal, they
~~~~ you la Boton —— the Mouse-colored
river where your neighbors
have fallen from each
other & gone down without
sleeping rage, or Monster looks
to ~~~~ — but as if
sleeping in the moon-quarried
room & the child gathers
her insects & startles

afternoon's spotterly ~~ensing~~ ~~~~ ~~~~ ~~~~ a child, ten parts ~~~~, woman, one part glass,
A Human different Painters ~~~~ ~~~~ l, ten parts this, Back a
single part ox blood, four parts asparagus
belief — return the umbrella
back to the periscope, the
stovepipe back to the crow,
the city-scape back to
the toy mountain, the lion
back to the girl, the
vault back —— to its contents, ~~~~
whose contents are not ~~~~ supported on tiny legs & little
by paper wings. I am trying to give you a real house, full
of real people. But the moon wasn't

TARPAULIN SKY PRESS
CURRENT AND FORTHCOMING TITLES

[one love affair]*, by Jenny Boully
Perfectbound & handbound editions

Body Language, by Mark Cunningham
Perfectbound & handbound editions

Attempts at a Life, by Danielle Dutton
Perfectbound & handbound editions

Figures for a Darkroom Voice,
by Noah Eli Gordon and Joshua Marie Wilkinson,
with images by Noah Saterstrom
Perfectbound & handbound editions

32 Pedals and 47 Stops, by Sandy Florian
Chapbook

Nylund, the Sarcographer, by Joyelle McSweeney
Perfectbound & handbound editions

Give Up, by Andrew Michael Roberts
Chapbook

A Mirror to Shatter the Hammer, by Chad Sweeney
Chapbook

The Pictures, by Max Winter
Perfectbound & handbound editions

www.tarpaulinsky.com